Rembrandt drew and painted amazing pictures of people.

One of his favorite subjects was his wife, Saskia.

Original Korean text by Haneul Ddang
Illustrations by Sam-hyeon Kim
Korean edition © Aram Publishing

This English edition published by big & SMALL in 2016
by arrangement with Aram Publishing
English text edited by Scott Forbes
English edition © big & SMALL 2016

Distributed in the United States and Canada by
Lerner Publishing Group, Inc.
241 First Avenue North
Minneapolis, MN 55401 U.S.A.
www.lernerbooks.com

ISBN: 978-1-925249-11-8

Printed in Korea

The Artist
and His Models

THE ART OF REMBRANDT

Written by Haneul Ddang
Illustrated by Sam-hyeon Kim
Edited by Scott Forbes

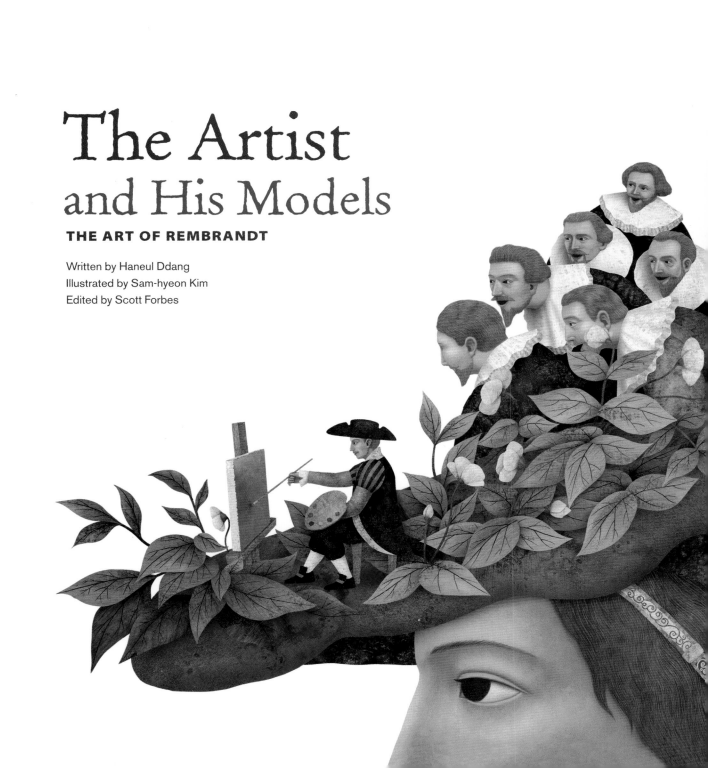

When Rembrandt painted people, he captured their gestures and their expressions precisely. And when those people saw themselves in his paintings, they were often astonished.

7

Once, some of the men in a work called *The Anatomy Lesson of Dr. Nicolaes Tulp* saw how cleverly he had painted them. "Look at my face," said one, "and how I am craning my neck to get a closer view. You can see how fascinated I was." "Oh dear," said another. "He noticed that I was bored and staring into space!"

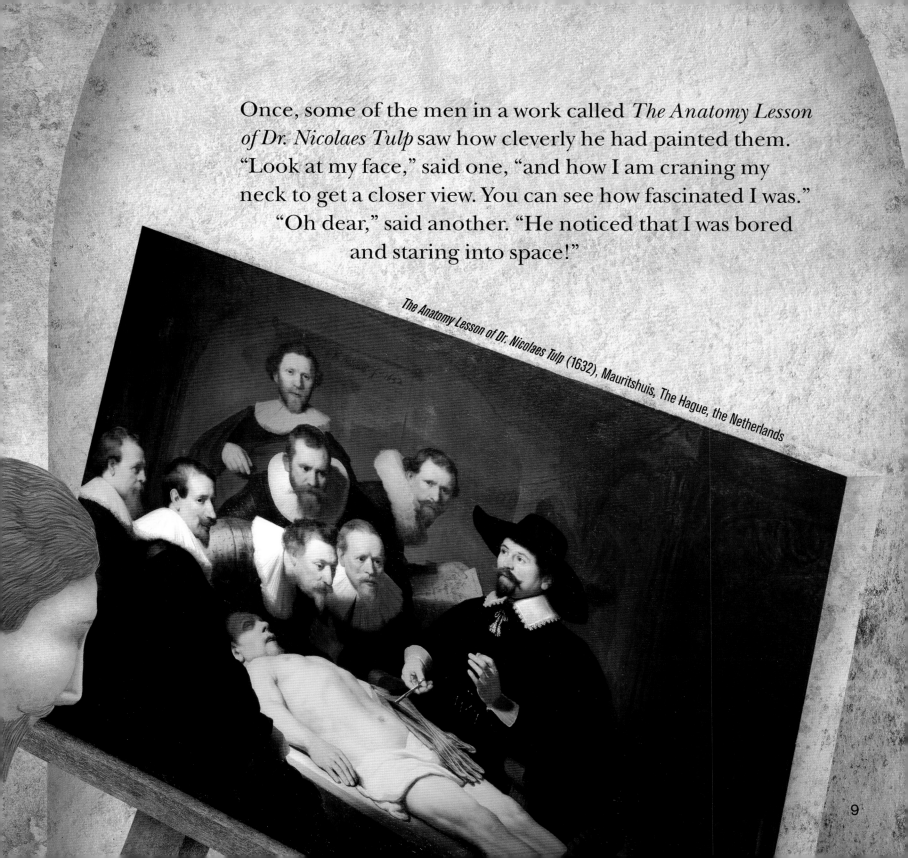

The Anatomy Lesson of Dr. Nicolaes Tulp (1632), Mauritshuis, The Hague, the Netherlands

9

For centuries before Rembrandt, artists had painted pictures of people. But often the people in these portraits look stern and stiff. They stare straight ahead as if they can't move or they are waiting for something to happen.

Rembrandt's paintings were different.
He often showed people doing things,
and expressed how they were feeling in that moment.

Because his paintings were so different, Rembrandt became successful when he was still quite young.

Portrait of George Villiers, First Duke of Buckingham (c. 1625)
by Peter Paul Rubens, Galleria Palatina, Florence, Italy

Portrait of Sir Thomas More (1527)
by Hans Holbein the Younger, Frick Collection, New York, USA

Portrait of Baldassare Castiglione (1514–15)
by Raphael, Louvre Museum, Paris, France

11

One day, Captain Banning Cocq, the leader
of the town guards, visited Rembrandt.
He asked him to make a painting of his company.
He said that he and 16 of the guards would pay for it.
He wanted a painting as lively as the one of Dr. Tulp.

Captain Cocq couldn't wait to see what Rembrandt would do.
Rembrandt was happy too, and promised himself
he would make it a very special painting.

Rembrandt worked on the painting for a long time.
He used a very large canvas and he painted many people.
They included Captain Cocq and the 16 guards who were
paying for the work. But he also painted some townspeople,
including a young girl who looked like his wife, Saskia, and
a man like Rembrandt himself.

Before Rembrandt finished
this picture, Saskia became
sick and died.
Rembrandt had lost
his favorite model.

15

The Night Watch (1642), Rijksmuseum,
Amsterdam, the Netherlands

16

Finally the painting of the guards was ready.
But many of the people who saw it didn't like it,
including some of those who were in it.

They said:
"It's too dark. You can't see me."
"Is that supposed to be me? I don't look like that, do I?"
"You can see only half of my face."
"I want my money back."
They were very unhappy.
Word spread that the painting was not a success.

Everything changed for Rembrandt after that.
People who had said they loved his work
no longer asked him to paint for them.
Few friends visited him. Rembrandt spent
most of his time alone.

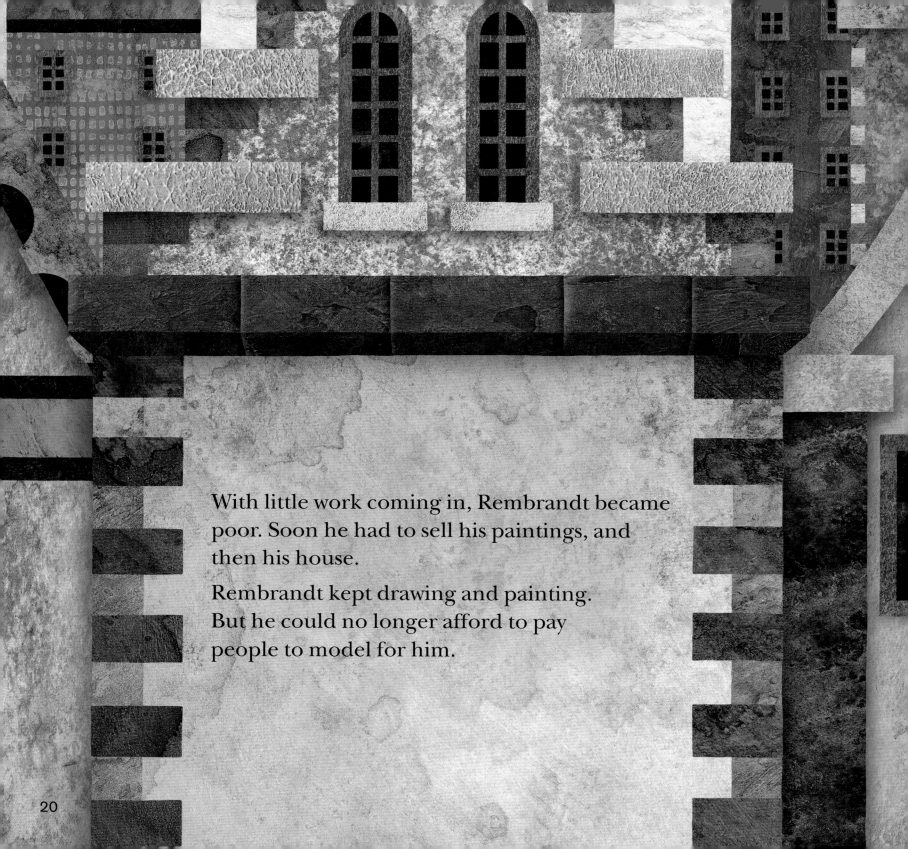

With little work coming in, Rembrandt became
poor. Soon he had to sell his paintings, and
then his house.

Rembrandt kept drawing and painting.
But he could no longer afford to pay
people to model for him.

Then one day a remarkable thing happened.
Rembrandt discovered a new model.
This model didn't even ask for any money
and was always available.

Rembrandt started to draw and paint his
new model all the time.
The model would stay with him for a long time —
in fact, until Rembrandt died.

As Rembrandt got older, so did his model.
This allowed Rembrandt to study a person ageing.
As he and his model aged, the paintings became
more and more special.
Rembrandt captured not just his model's changing face,
but also a sense of how he was feeling and of the life he had lived.

These late paintings were marvellous works,
unlike those of any other artist.
Rembrandt died poor. But in his art he had achieved
what he had set out to do. He had painted real people
in a way that expressed their feelings and emotions.

Self-portrait as the Apostle Paul (1662),
Rijksmuseum, Amsterdam,
the Netherlands

Self-portrait as a Young Man (1634),
Uffizi Gallery, Florence, Italy

Saskia with a Red Flower (1634), Staatliche Kunstsammlungen, Dresden, Germany

26

Half-length Figure of Saskia in a Red Hat
(1634), Schloss Wilhelmshöhe,
Kassel, Germany

Throughout his life, Rembrandt painted
many people. But two models were
most important to him.
One was his dear wife, Saskia,
who left him all too soon.

27

And that other model, who aged alongside
Rembrandt and stayed with him until the very end?
Why, that was none other than Rembrandt himself!

Self-portrait as Zeuxis Laughing (1663),
Wallfraf-Richartz-Museum,
Cologne, Germany

29

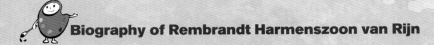
Master of the portrait

Self-portrait as a Young Man (1634), Uffizi Gallery, Florence, Italy

Rembrandt was born in the town of Leiden in the Netherlands, in northeastern Europe, in 1606. He was an artist who experienced many ups and downs in his life.

Rembrandt showed artistic talent at an early age. As a young man, he studied under the artist Jacob van Swanenburgh for three years. Then he studied with other artists in Leiden and Amsterdam before setting up his own studio in Leiden in 1625.

To practice and develop his art, Rembrandt drew many local people, from passersby in the street to elderly neighbors. He also taught other people to draw. Gradually he developed his own particular style.

Most of Rembrandt's paintings are of people. Some are portraits of individuals, while others show large groups. The people in Rembrandt's paintings often seem like actors on a stage because their faces are usually lit up by bright light and are so expressive.

Early success

Rembrandt's art steadily became more popular. By the time he was in his mid-30s, he was considered Leiden's best artist. Students crowded into his studio to learn from him. Wealthy clients lined up to place orders for paintings.

Rembrandt had all the money and success he desired. But, unfortunately, these happy times did not last long.

Half-length Figure of Saskia in a Red Hat (1634),
Schloss Wilhelmshöhe, Kassel, Germany

One misfortune after another

In 1634, Rembrandt married Saskia van
Uylenburgh. Their first three children – two
sons and a daughter – died soon after they
were born. Only their fourth son, Titus,
lived to become an adult.

Then, in 1642, Saskia died. After losing
three children, this was almost too much
for Rembrandt to bear. But he decided he
had to keep working hard to support Titus.
Sadly, at this time too, Rembrandt's
business began to fail. He ran out of
money and had to sell his house and
many of his possessions.

His most reliable model

Fewer people asked Rembrandt for
paintings and he struggled to make a
living. At one point he became so poor
that he didn't have money for firewood.
But the hardest part of being poor for
Rembrandt was not being able to buy
paints or pay models to sit for him.

Yet, even though he led a hard life,
Rembrandt kept on drawing and painting.
He studied and painted his own face, over
and over. He himself became the best
model he could have hoped for.

Self-portrait as Zeuxis Laughing (1663), Wallfraf-Richartz-
Museum, Cologne, Germany

1606
Born in Leiden, in what
is now the Netherlands

1621
Begins to study under
the artist Jacob van
Swanenburgh

1625
Sets up his own
studio in Leiden

1630s
Becomes famous as
a portrait painter

1634
Marries Saskia van
Uylenburgh

1642
Saskia dies soon after
the birth of a son, Titus

1657
Rembrandt sells his
house to pay his debts

1669
One year after the death
of his son Titus, Rembrandt
dies alone. He is buried in
an unmarked grave.

A group portrait

In Rembrandt's time, paintings of several people together, known as group portraits, were very popular. In 1632, Rembrandt was asked to paint a famous doctor, Dr. Tulp, and the people who came to hear his lectures in Amsterdam on anatomy – the study of the human body. Rembrandt didn't want to paint them simply standing in a line, looking at the artist. Instead he decided to show one of the doctor's lectures as it was happening.

When the painting was completed, it was hung in a large assembly hall, where important people gathered. The men in the painting were very satisfied when they saw it.

Rembrandt had captured their intense interest in the lecture. The expressions on their faces showed that they were fascinated and amazed by what the doctor was telling them about the human body.

Rembrandt gave the painting a dark background, so that viewers would focus on the men and their expressions.

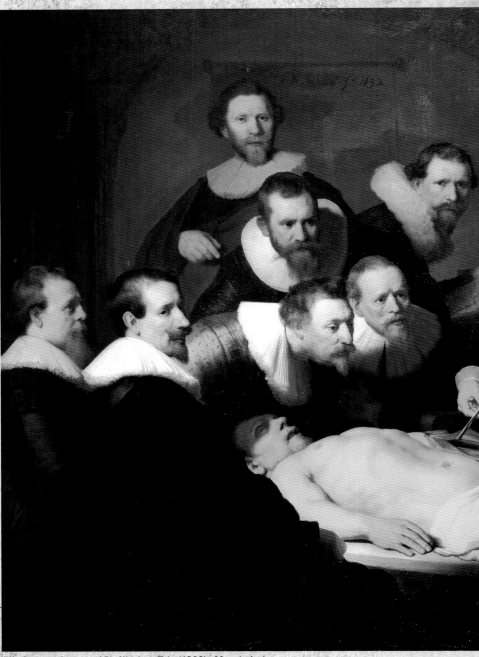

The Anatomy Lesson of Dr. Nicolaes Tulp (1632), Mauritshuis, The Hague, the Netherlands

Dr. Tulp is at the right, speaking to his audience. He is describing the muscles and nerves in the human arm. Rembrandt gave the doctor a wide-brimmed hat so that he would stand out from the other people in the portrait.

The painting was a great success and made many people curious about the study of anatomy.

The book at the bottom right is the anatomy textbook doctors used in Rembrandt's time.

The body in the picture is that of a thief called Aris Kindt, who had been executed for his crimes. His body was then donated to the Amsterdam Guild of Surgeons to be used for teaching. In Rembrandt's time only the bodies of criminals could be used for this purpose.

Rembrandt's two favorite models: